HEROES OF MEDICINE AND THEIR DISCOVERIES

Angela Royston

Crabtree Publishing Company

www.crabtreebooks.com

Author: Angela Royston
Editor: Kathy Middleton
Production coordinator: Ken Wright
Prepress technician: Margaret Amy Salter
Series consultant: Gill Matthews

Picture Credits:
Bayer Business Services: Corporate History & Archives 22t, 22b
Corbis: Bettmann 27
Courtesy of the National Library of Medicine: 7b, 8, 13, 14, 18, 19, 21, 23
Getty Images: Hulton Archive 10
Library of Congress: 9t, 20t
National Archives: 25b
Photolibrary: 24
Public Health Image Library: CDC/Jean Roy 9b, CDC/Don Stalons 25t
Shutterstock: Cover, Oguz Aral 6, Linda Bucklin 5t, Condor36 29, Daisy Daisy 26, Christian Darkin 15b, Jubal Harshaw 15t, Girish Menon 5b, Dario Sabljak 20b, MichaelTaylor 17
Wikimedia Commons: 7t, 11, 16, Ernest Board 12, Rick Proser 28, Peter Treveris 4

The medical procedures described in this book were carried out in the past and should not be attempted today.

Every effort has been made to trace copyright holders and to obtain their permission for use of copyright material. The authors and publishers would be pleased to rectify any error or omission in future editions. All the Internet addresses given in this book were correct at the time of going to press. The author and publishers regret any inconvenience caused if addresses have changed or sites have ceased to exist, but can accept no responsibility for any such changes.

Library and Archives Canada Cataloguing in Publication

Royston, Angela
    Heroes of medicine and their discoveries / Angela Royston.

(Crabtree connections)
Includes index.
ISBN 978-0-7787-9897-2 (bound).--ISBN 978-0-7787-9918-4 (pbk.)

        1. Medical innovations--Juvenile literature.
2. Inventors--Juvenile literature.
I. Title. II. Series: Crabtree connections.

RA418.5.M4R69 2011   j610   C2010-905298-6

Library of Congress Cataloging-in-Publication Data

Royston, Angela, 1945-
    Heroes of medicine and their discoveries / Angela Royston.
        p. cm. -- (Crabtree connections)
    Includes index.
    ISBN 978-0-7787-9918-4 (pbk. : alk. paper) -- ISBN 978-0-7787-9897-2 (reinforced library binding : alk. paper)
    1. Medical innovations--Juvenile literature. I. Title.
    RA418.5.M4R69 2011
    610.92'2--dc22

                        2010032437

Crabtree Publishing Company

www.crabtreebooks.com   1-800-387-7650

Copyright © 2011 **CRABTREE PUBLISHING COMPANY.**
All rights reserved. No part of this publication may be reproduced, stored in a retrieval system or be transmitted in any form or by any means, electronic, mechanical, photocopying, recording, or otherwise, without the prior written permission of Crabtree Publishing Company. Published in the United Kingdom in 2010 by A & C Black Publishers Ltd. The right of the author of this work has been asserted.

Printed in the U.S.A./082010/WO20101210

Published in Canada
Crabtree Publishing
616 Welland Ave.
St. Catharines, Ontario
L2M 5V6

Published in the United States
Crabtree Publishing
PMB 59051
350 Fifth Avenue, 59th Floor
New York, New York 10118

Contents

Good News

▼ Trepanning was believed to relieve pressure on the brain, but it was quite gruesome!

People are excited when a scientist discovers a new treatment for an illness or an injury. A medical breakthrough can lead to better ways of curing people.

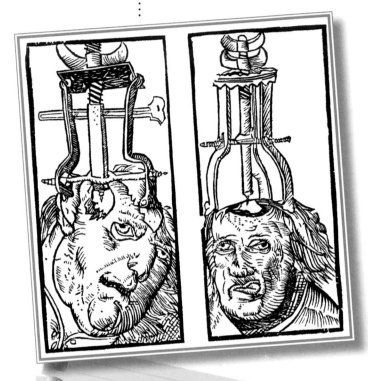

DEADLY DISEASES

Four hundred years ago, doctors had few ways of helping sick people. People died from illnesses, such as scarlet fever, that are easily cured today. Doctors did not understand how people caught diseases, so they could not prevent them.

~~BORING CURE~~ **BAD IDEA**

People have been trying to cure disease since prehistoric times. Ancient skulls have been found with holes **bored** through them. The holes were bored while the person was still alive. This is called **trepanning**. It was done to let out evil spirits, which people believed caused illness and pain.

4

FATAL WOUNDS

Injuries, such as bad cuts and broken bones, were often fatal because the wounds became infected. Doctors did not understand what caused **infection** and could not cure it.

TESTING CURES

Some cures did more harm than good, until scientists and doctors realized that they had to test their ideas and cures to see if they worked. Today, new medicines have to be tested for several years before they are used on sick people.

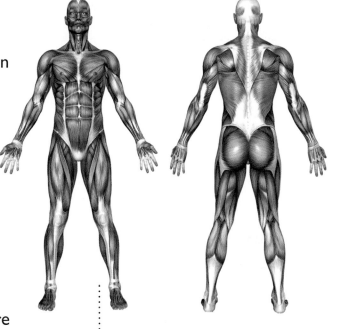

▲ Observing the inside of the human body helped surgeons to understand how it works.

▼ Surgeons operate on a person in a hospital. The machines and techniques used now were once medical breakthroughs.

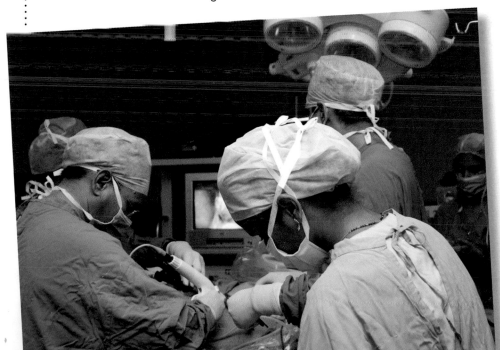

The Heart Is Just a Pump

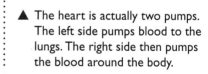

Dr. William Harvey, the doctor to King Charles I, has just published an astonishing idea. He says that the heart pumps blood around the body.

A REVOLUTIONARY IDEA!

According to Dr. Harvey, blood leaves the heart through the **arteries** and returns through the **veins**. "The movement of blood occurs constantly, in a circular manner," he claims.

▲ The heart is actually two pumps. The left side pumps blood to the lungs. The right side then pumps the blood around the body.

PRECIOUS HEART

The Egyptians thought that their heart held their soul and was where their thoughts and feelings came from. When someone died, the body and heart were **mummified**, but the brain was thrown away.

6

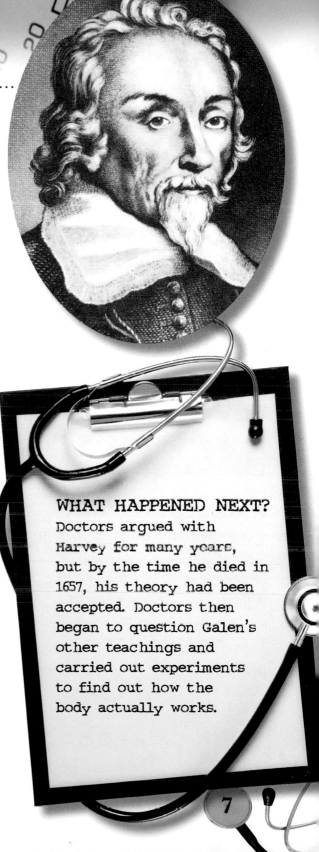

DOCTORS SAY THAT HARVEY IS MAD

"He is crack-brained," says Jean Riolan, France's leading doctor. Like other doctors, Riolan follows the ancient teachings of Galen. He was a doctor who treated **gladiators** and four Roman **emperors** 1,500 years ago.

▼ This drawing by Dr. Harvey shows that arteries and veins have **valves** that allow blood to flow in one direction only.

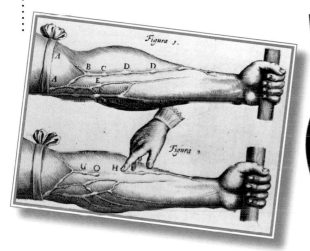

WHO IS RIGHT?

Galen said that blood is made in the liver. As it travels through the body, it is used up. But Dr. Harvey insists that his experiments on living and dead animals, such as deer, prove that blood moves continuously around the body and is not used up.

WHAT HAPPENED NEXT?

Doctors argued with Harvey for many years, but by the time he died in 1657, his theory had been accepted. Doctors then began to question Galen's other teachings and carried out experiments to find out how the body actually works.

7

No More Pock Marks

1796

Dr. Edward Jenner has found a way to protect people from smallpox. He calls it inoculation. Is this the end of the terrible disease?

▲ Dr. Edward Jenner

COWPOX

Every dairymaid knows that she will never catch smallpox if she has already caught cowpox from milking cows. Cowpox is similar to smallpox, but milder, and it can pass from cows to people. Dr. Jenner developed his inoculation using pus from cowpox blisters.

HORRORS OF SMALLPOX

In 400 AD, a medical book from India described a disease in which "the pustules are red, yellow, and white, and they are accompanied by burning pain." The disease was probably smallpox. Smallpox killed about 80 percent of children who caught it.

Dairymaids do not have **pock marks**. ▶
They have clear skin, because they
do not catch smallpox.

THE FIRST INJECTION

James Phipps, an eight-year-old boy, was
one of the first people to be inoculated.
On May 14, 1796, Jenner scratched
James's arms with pus from a cowpox
blister. Then on July 1, Jenner infected
James with pus from a smallpox blister.
James did not catch smallpox. The
inoculation worked!

▼ This boy's skin is covered in smallpox
blisters. Dr. Jenner believes smallpox
may be wiped out thanks to inoculation.

WHAT HAPPENED NEXT?

People around the world
were **vaccinated**, when
they realized that Jenner's
inoculation worked. In
1801, Jenner said, "the
annihilation of the Small
Pox . . . must be the final
result of [vaccination]."
It was not until 1980,
however, that smallpox
was wiped out.

Embarrassed Doctor Invents Stethoscope

1816

French doctor René Laennec has invented an instrument for listening to a patient's heart. It is called a stethoscope, and he has invented it to avoid embarrassment!

REVEALING SOUNDS

William Harvey (see page 6) said that the heart should sound like "two clacks of a **water bellows**." Doctors also listen to the patient's breathing to see if they can hear liquid in the breathing tubes.

10

How Life Begins

Nearly twenty years ago, this newspaper reported the amazing fact that every living thing is made up of tiny cells. Now, German scientist Rudolf Virchow has discovered that every cell comes from another living cell!

▲ Rudolf Virchow

DISCOVERY OF CELLS

In 1838, two German scientists, Theodor Schwann and Matthias Schleiden, realized that all living things—both plants and animals—are made up of tiny cells. Schwann thought that cells formed from a non-living substance, which he called "blastema." He was wrong!

LOGICAL CONCLUSION

In 1883, scientist August Weisman pointed out that, if all cells come from preexisting cells, then all cells "can trace their **ancestry** back to ancient times." In other words, every living thing could be descended from one original cell!

TOO CLOSE FOR COMFORT

For centuries, doctors have listened to the heart beating by putting their ear to the patient's chest. Laennec could not bring himself to do this to a young woman patient. Instead, he grabbed several sheets of paper and rolled them up. He put one end of the roll of paper on the woman's chest and his ear to the other end. He knew the sound of her heartbeat would pass along the rolled tube, but he was amazed to hear her heart even louder and clearer than usual!

WHAT HAPPENED NEXT?

Laennec made a stethoscope from wood, and used it to study diseases, such as pneumonia and tuberculosis. The stethoscope has since become one of the most important instruments for doctors. Diseases can be more easily **diagnosed** by examining **symptoms** through a stethoscope.

▼ Dr. Laennec uses his stethoscope to listen to a boy's lungs.

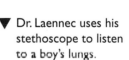

We Have Conquered Pain!

The first painless operation took place at Massachusetts General Hospital yesterday. William Morton used an anesthetic—a gas that saves the patient from the agonizing pain of a major operation.

▼ William Morton is shown anesthetizing his patient.

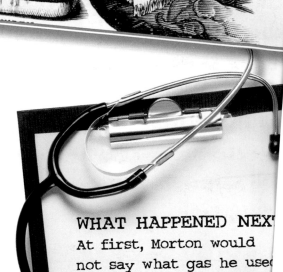

This patient is being ▶ anesthetized—he is not yet unconscious!

EXTRAORDINARY DEMONSTRATION

Before surgeon John Collins Warren removed a **tumor** from Edward Abbott's neck, Morton gave Abbott a gas to breathe in. The gas kept him **unconscious** throughout the operation. When he recovered, Abbott claimed that he had felt nothing, no pain at all. Doctors and medical students watched Warren carry out this extraordinary event.

OPERATING WITHOUT ANESTHETICS

Morton's new discovery means that patients will no longer scream in agony during operations. Until now, most patients were simply held down while operations were carried out. Some were punched unconscious, while others were given alcohol or **opium**. But nothing fully deadened the pain.

WHAT HAPPENED NEXT

At first, Morton would not say what gas he used. But once he admitted that it was ether, the use of anesthetics spread fast. Just a few months after the demonstration, the *People's Journal* in London exclaimed, "We have conquered pain."

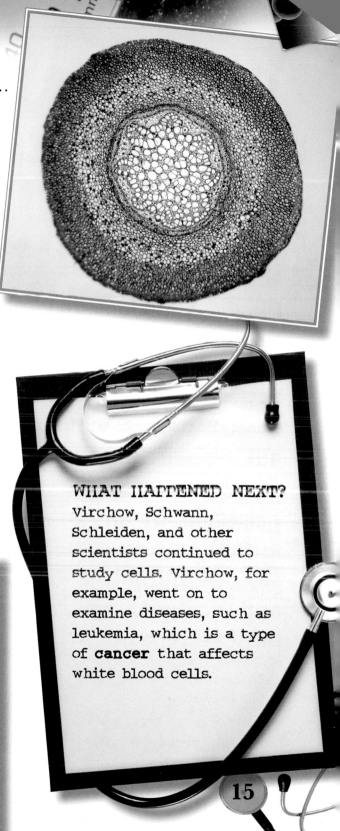

This slice through the root of a fern has been **magnified** to show that it is made of cells.

THE NEW THEORY

Virchow's new book describes how existing cells divide to form new cells. "Every cell comes from another living cell," he says. Even more amazing is his claim that every individual grows from a single cell. This first cell divides over and over again to form all the cells in the body.

▼ An amoeba is a tiny animal made up of just one animal cell. Amoebas are blobs that can easily change shape.

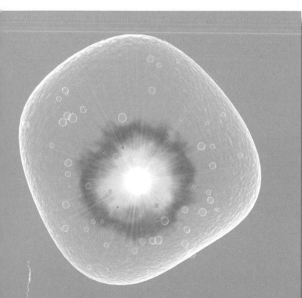

WHAT HAPPENED NEXT?
Virchow, Schwann, Schleiden, and other scientists continued to study cells. Virchow, for example, went on to examine diseases, such as leukemia, which is a type of **cancer** that affects white blood cells.

15

Germs All Around Us

Finally, Louis Pasteur has proved that germs exist! This great French scientist has argued for years that germs exist and are all around us, but other scientists insulted and mocked him— until yesterday.

Louis Pasteur is shown ▶
at work in his laboratory.

WINNING THE ARGUMENT

In 1854, Pasteur was asked to find out why some beer and wine turns sour and has to be thrown away. But when he announced in 1857 that tiny living things, called microbes or germs, do the damage, no one believed him. Yesterday, however, Pasteur invited a group of famous scientists to the University of Paris. He proved to them beyond a doubt that germs do exist, and they can be killed by heat.

WHAT HAPPENED NEXT?

Louis Pasteur believed that some diseases, such as cholera and typhoid, were caused by germs. Following Jenner (see page 8), he tried to create vaccines against these diseases. By 1885 he had a vaccine against rabies. Today there are vaccines against most deadly diseases.

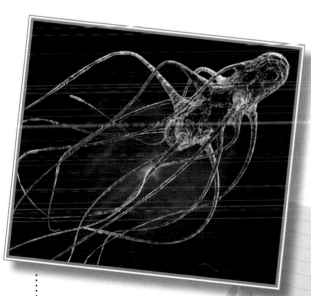

▲ A single salmonella bacteria is revealed under a microscope. Salmonella is a form of food poisoning.

PRESERVING MILK

Untreated milk turns sour quickly. Pasteur showed that, if milk is heated, germs are killed and the milk stays good. This process came to be known as pasteurization.

17

Carbolic Acid Kills Germs

1867

Surgeon Joseph Lister has saved a 13-year-old's badly wounded arm by washing it with carbolic acid! The arm has now healed. Lister claims this is because the dangerous acid killed the germs in the wound.

▲ Joseph Lister

DEADLY ROT

Hospital wards that do not use **antiseptic** smell like the rotting wounds of patients. Without antiseptic, nearly half of all patients who had to have a limb amputated died, because the wounds became infected with germs.

THE ACCIDENT

When the boy was brought into Glasgow Royal Infirmary, his arm was badly cut and the bones were broken. Lister says that he would normally have amputated the arm at the shoulder. Because he knew how to use antiseptic carbolic acid, however, he did not hesitate to try to save the limb.

▼ Lister has used carbolic acid during operations since 1865. It helped wounds heal, which otherwise would have become infected.

WHAT HAPPENED NEXT?
As well as using carbolic acid during surgery, Lister made his surgeons wash their hands and spray their instruments with carbolic acid. His methods were so successful, other hospitals also used them, and surgery became much safer.

X-ray—the Invisible Ray

Wilhelm Conrad Röntgen has discovered an invisible ray. The ray is called an X-ray, and it can photograph bones inside the body!

This X-ray shows ▶ a skull and the bones at the top of the spine.

▲ German scientist Wilhelm Conrad Röntgen

20

DISCOVERED BY ACCIDENT

Röntgen discovered the rays by accident. On November 8, 1895, he was experimenting with a **cathode ray** tube that had been tightly covered with black cardboard. The room was dark and he noticed that, whenever he passed electricity through the tube, a piece of photographic paper lying nearby glowed. He concluded that invisible rays were passing from the tube through the cardboard, making the **chemical** on the paper glow.

METAL AND BONES

Röntgen investigated the rays for several weeks. He found that they could pass through most things, even a thick book. On December 22, he passed the rays through his wife's hand. They created a shadow of the bones in her hand and her two rings, because only the bones and the metal had blocked the rays.

WHAT HAPPENED NEXT? Röntgen published his discovery in a German scientific journal on December 28, 1895, and the news spread fast around the world. Today, X-ray machines are used by doctors and dentists everywhere to examine bones and teeth.

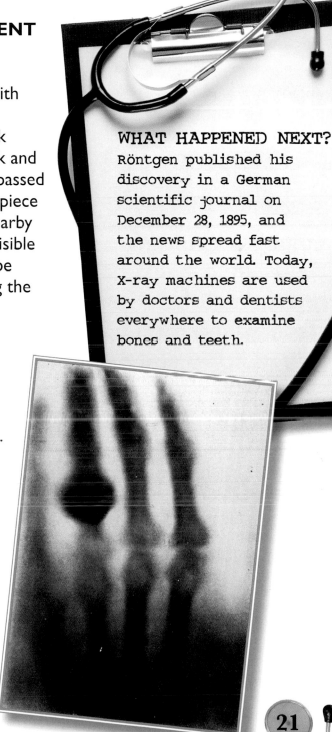

The very first X-ray shows ▶ Röntgen's wife's hand.

21

Wonder Drug Discovered

1899

A wonderful new medicine has just been launched. It is called Aspirin, and it relieves severe aches and pains!

SURPRISE DISCOVERY

The drug was made by Felix Hoffmann, a German chemist. He added a group of chemicals called acetyl to salicylic acid. Salicylic acid is known to reduce pain, but Hoffman was surprised to find that the new medicine reduces swelling, too. It also lowers the high temperature of patients with **fever**. Hoffman's father is one person who will benefit from the new medicine. He suffers severe pain due to **rheumatism**.

Powdered Aspirin is now available in bottles! ▶

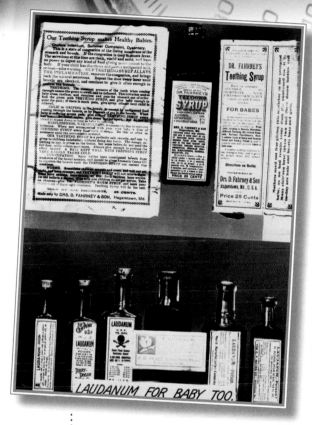

Our Teething Syrup makes Healthy Babies.

DR. FAHRNEY'S Teething Syrup

FOR BABES

▲ Laudanum is now available for babies too!

CENTURIES-OLD REMEDY

Some plants contain natural salicin. For centuries they have been ground up and taken to relieve pain. However, salicin irritates the stomach, so the pure acid is only given to people who, like Hoffman's father, are in extreme pain.

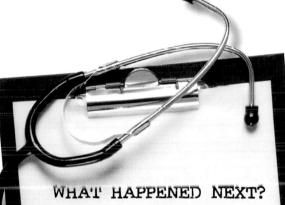

~~LAUDANUM~~
BAD IDEA

Laudanum is a form of opium and is now illegal, or against the law. Before Aspirin, however, many people took laudanum to deaden toothaches and other kinds of pain. Mothers even gave it to babies to stop them from crying when they were teething.

WHAT HAPPENED NEXT?

Aspirin was first sold as a powder in a bottle, but was later sold in pill form. It is one of the most famous medicines of all time. Today, however, doctors are concerned that Aspirin is not safe for children, so they are given other painkillers.

Miracle Cure

The Nobel Prize for Medicine has been awarded to these three great scientists— Alexander Fleming, Howard Florey, and Ernst Chain—for the discovery and development of penicillin.

▲ Fleming, Florey, and Chain are presented with the Nobel Prize for Medicine in Sweden.

BACTERIA KILLER

"When I woke up on September 28, 1928," said Alexander Fleming, "I certainly didn't plan to revolutionize medicine by discovering the world's first antibiotic, or bacteria killer." But that is exactly what he did.

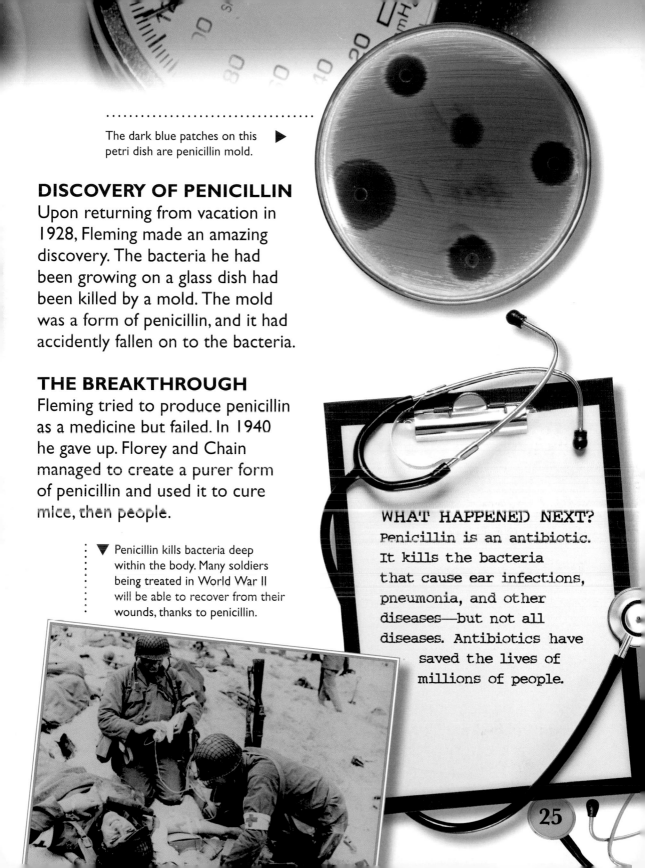

The dark blue patches on this petri dish are penicillin mold. ▶

DISCOVERY OF PENICILLIN

Upon returning from vacation in 1928, Fleming made an amazing discovery. The bacteria he had been growing on a glass dish had been killed by a mold. The mold was a form of penicillin, and it had accidently fallen on to the bacteria.

THE BREAKTHROUGH

Fleming tried to produce penicillin as a medicine but failed. In 1940 he gave up. Florey and Chain managed to create a purer form of penicillin and used it to cure mice, then people.

▼ Penicillin kills bacteria deep within the body. Many soldiers being treated in World War II will be able to recover from their wounds, thanks to penicillin.

WHAT HAPPENED NEXT?
Penicillin is an antibiotic. It kills the bacteria that cause ear infections, pneumonia, and other diseases—but not all diseases. Antibiotics have saved the lives of millions of people.

25

MRI Scanner Sees Everything

1977

An amazing new machine, called an MRI scanner, will allow doctors to see everything inside the body. Unlike an X-ray, which shows only hard bones, an MRI scan shows all the soft parts, such as the brain, too. It even shows cancer tumors.

▼ An MRI scan of a person's brain

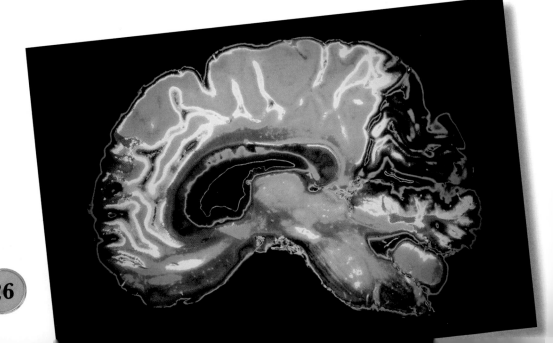

INDOMITABLE

American doctor Raymond Damadian has created a machine that can scan humans for diseases such as cancer. In 1970, Damadian first noticed that a machine that combines **radio waves** and **magnetism** could detect cancer tumors in rats. Other scientists did not think it would work, but Damadian has spent the last seven years building his own scanner. He calls it *Indomitable*.

▲ Damadian explains how his MRI scanner works.

THE FIRST SCAN

On July 3, 1977, Damadian and his team carried out the first human body scan. It took four hours and 45 minutes, but it produced a clear picture of the heart, lungs, and chest. It has convinced his colleagues that the machine will work.

STRANGE EXPERIENCE

Having a scan can feel strange. The patient lies on a table, which then moves into the scanner's narrow tunnel. The tunnel is hot and the machine is very noisy. Some scans take 30 to 40 minutes, but others are done in seconds.

WHAT HAPPENED NEXT?

MRI scanners now work faster and have been used in hospitals around the world since the 1980s. They are used to diagnose many kinds of problems from strained muscles to tumors in the brain.

New Hearts in the Future

Today

In France, **Professor Alain Carpentier has invented an artificial heart. "I couldn't stand seeing young, active people, aged 40, dying from massive heart attacks," he said. He has spent nearly 20 years developing the artificial heart. He expects it to be ready to use in patients by 2011.**

NEW HEARTS NEEDED

Heart failure kills up to 17 million people worldwide every year. These people desperately need new hearts. Different groups of scientists are working hard to produce entirely new hearts.

▲ One of the first artificial hearts ever made is shown above.

▲ Surgeons operate on a patient's heart to make it work better. When a heart is very damaged, it is difficult to keep it working.

HEART TRANSPLANTS

In 1967, South African doctor Christiaan Barnard carried out the first successful **heart transplant** on patient Louis Washkansky. Since then, heart transplants have become common, but there are not enough hearts for everyone who needs them. This is why scientists are developing other solutions.

WHAT WILL HAPPEN NEXT?

Scientists in Australia have already grown new healthy, heart muscle from a small piece of existing heart muscle. Meanwhile, scientists in the United States have grown new skin and new bone, using existing skin and bone.

29

Glossary

annihilation Complete destruction

ancestry Line of ancestors before you

antiseptic Substance that kills germs

arteries Tubes that carry blood away from the heart

bored Made a hole with a piercing tool

cancer Disease in which cells in the body grow out of control

cathode ray Stream of electrically charged particles

cells Smallest building blocks of living things

chemical Powerful substance found in both natural and man-made things

diagnose To identify a disease

emperors Men who rule empires

fever Very high body temperature

germs Tiny living things that can cause disease

gladiators People who fought in public arenas during Roman times

heart transplant To transfer a living heart from one body to another

indomitable Not able to be conquered

infection Disease caused by germs

inoculation Making a person able to resist a disease by infecting them with mild or dead germs

magnetism Forces of attraction and repulsion made by magnets

magnified Enlarged to an extreme measure

opium Powerful drug

penicillin Drug made from a mold that can kill bacteria

pock marks Scars left on the skin after blisters have healed

radio waves Form of energy produced by combining electricity and magnetism

ray Beam of energy

rheumatism Painful disease that affects the joints

smallpox A virus passed from person to person that covers the skin in pus-filled blisters

symptoms Signs or evidence of an illness

trepanning To drill holes in the skull to relieve pressure

tumor Growth or swelling on the body

unconscious Loss of awareness and feeling

vaccinated Given a vaccine in order to protect against disease

valves Something in the body that act like doors allowing substances through in one direction but not the other

veins Tubes that carry blood back to the heart

water bellows Water-aided device for delivering pressurized air

Further Information

WEB SITES
Search for information about different inventions in the National Inventors Hall of Fame at:
www.invent.org/hall_of_fame/1_1_search.asp

Explore a wealth of inventor and invention resources at:
http://web.mit.edu/invent/iow/i-archive-mh.html

Read about the greatest medical breakthroughs of all time at:
http://science.discovery.com/convergence/100discoveries/big100/ medicine.html

Find more great information about scientific breakthroughs in medicine at:
www.kidskonnect.com/subject-index/15-science/ 86-inventors-a-inventions.html

BOOKS
Medical Breakthroughs (Graphic Discoveries) by Gary Jeffrey and Terry Riley. Rosen Classroom (2007).

The 10 Most Significant Medical Breakthroughs by Denis Carr. Children's Press (2008).

Index